DISCOVER THE MAGIC OF EFT FOR BULLYING

DISCOVER THE MAGIC OF EFT FOR BULLYING

Debby Guddee

Illustrations by Su Mon

Cover designer: Haresh R. Makwana

Library of Congress Control Number: 2014909209

ISBN 13   978-1-500 1-9528-1
ISBN 10   1-5001-9528-6

First Published for Create Space: 06/22/2014

Disclaimer

The content within this book is educational only and is not to be deemed as or used as a substitute for any medical or psychological advice or care. If in doubt always consult your medical or health practitioner.

This book introduces you to a self-help method known as EFT (emotional freedom techniques) otherwise known as energy medicine. EFT works on the basis that the body is made up of energy, and when that energy is out of balance, distress occurs, and by correcting the energy imbalance, the distress goes away.

Whilst EFT has produced (and continues to produce) remarkable clinical results over its many years, it must still be considered in the experimental stage, and therefore, whoever chooses to use this method must take full and complete responsibility for its use.

It is recommended that children under the age of eighteen are to use this book with adult supervision and suggest that the use of these techniques is done in conjunction with existing medical or psychological advice or care.

The characters in this book are purely fictional, and the views and experiences are those of the author, which at no time diminish from those that any individual may be experiencing.

Contents

Introduction

Bullying is happening everywhere, and according to the Kandersteg Declaration Against Bullying in Children and Youth, an estimated 200 million children around the world are being bullied, which is quite staggering. Unfortunately, bullying can often be something that is suffered in silence as the young person lives in fear of what may happen if they speak up.

Unfortunately, if the young person cannot successfully find a way to feel better about being bullied, this could lead to more serious issues in later life, such as depression or low self-esteem, and according to Centre for Adolescent Health, children who are bullied are three times more likely to show depressive symptoms than those who are not.

I myself was bullied throughout my school years between the ages eleven to sixteen where I was subject to both verbal and physical bullying, having been pinched, punched, called horrible names, had handfuls of hair pulled out, and continually kicked and tormented, but rarely, if ever, in front of my friends or any teachers.

This was an extremely stressful and anxious time, and during it all I had little to no idea why it was happening to *me*. Many years later, I came to think that it may have been because I was different, and that I almost always wore secondhand clothes, had a large group of friends, and was fairly good at most things, so trust me, I do know what it's like. Unfortunately for me, bullying continued long after I left school and followed me into the workplace, where I experienced intimidating and covert bullying.

EFT (emotional freedom techniques), otherwise known as *tapping,* helped me overcome this, and I'm happy to say that it is now out of my life for good, and through this experience I have gained the confidence to stand up to bullying and have also achieved a healthy self-esteem. However, by personally going through these experiences, it has given me a great desire to help others and write this book in the hope of helping and encouraging many children to also overcome the devastating effects of bullying, and give them the confidence that there is help out there, and also that there is something that can quickly help them feel better.

I respect and understand that there are many ways to deal with bullying situations; however, this book is written solely from the point of view of using EFT and in no way undermines any other method. In fact I would encourage you to use EFT along with any and all other help and resources that you have available to you. However, I do know that EFT will help you *feel* better, and by feeling better, it enables you to get back your own power and confidence, which means that bullies will no longer have any hold over you, which then frees you from the effects of being bullied.

Other EFT books have been written for adults and children, and although extremely popular books, people still seem to lack the understanding of when and how to use EFT, and what to do with it. Discover the Magic of EFT clearly demonstrates how to do this through a situation within a story and how easily tapping can be used.

This book gives children the opportunity to *do* something and take control of what can often feel like a helpless or vulnerable situation and provides a coping mechanism which they can use at any time, in or out of school.

All in all, this all makes for an extremely powerful and positive experience.

I would love for you to share your success stories and how, through Discovering the Magic of EFT, this book has helped you with bullying.

This book is the first in a series of many, other topics will be covered in future *Discover the Magic of EFT* books.

What is EFT?

EFT is quite magical, and you don't need to believe in magic for it to work.

It is known as *an emotional form of acupuncture*; however, there are no needles involved as it uses the fingers to lightly tap on certain parts of the face and body while thinking about, and feeling, an unhappy situation. You can have someone tap for you or you can tap for yourself. For example, if you tap when you are feeling sad or angry, after a short time (approximately twenty minutes) you will feel better; it's that simple. All you need to do is *give it a try and don't ask why.*

It works with our body's natural electrical circuit, with the understanding that when we experience something that cause us distress, energy gets *stuck* at certain points in this circuit. It is not a painful thing to happen but it does mean that energy cannot flow freely, think of it like water trying to get through a blocked pipe. This *stuck energy* can remain in the body for a long time until you find a way to release it. You will know if this is happening as when you think about something in the past and you feel unhappy or angry about it, you can bet it will be the stuck energy that is causing you to feel this

11

way. All you need to do is dissolve it and you will feel better; it's as simple and easy as that!

EFT tapping helps to clear stuck energy quickly and easily, which means that when you tap when thinking about what has caused you to feel distress, you will no longer feel angry or worry about it. In fact it's very likely that it won't bother you at all, which means that the things a bully has said or done will no longer matter, and you will be on your way to gaining confidence and achieving a healthy self-esteem. Just like magic!

I would like to add that, although EFT is highly effective when used as outlined in this book, it might not stop the bullying straight away, but because you feel better about it and the bully gets no reaction from you, they are likely to stop bullying you.

As mentioned previously, EFT is very easy to learn and do, it is quick and painless, and once you know it, you can use it over and over.

One thing I would say is that I wish I could have had the opportunity to know about it when I was going through my bullying time as I could have overcome it myself so much earlier and probably also would not have been bullied in the workplace.

With this book in your hands, you now have the opportunity to do just that and create your own personal magic.

Notes For Parents, Teachers or Caregivers

This book has been written with many parts to it.

The main part is a short story which is an introduction on how the magic of EFT works. It has been written to help the young person identify with the bullying issue experienced as the character takes them on their own journey of what they may be going through themselves and demonstrates how easy EFT can be used for their own situation.

Within the story, selected words and phrases are used as a *tapping script* which forms a guide to work with the young person as the book is read out loud, or for the young person to read it themselves and tap along with.

Although the name of the character in the story is female, you may change the name and gender of the character to suit your name, or that of the person you are reading the book to.

This book focuses on the four major aspects of bullying:

- *Verbal Bullying* - which includes name-calling, insults,

teasing, intimidation, homophobic or racist remarks, and verbal abuse.

- *Intimidating or Covert Bullying* - this is often done behind the child's back. It consists of the bully spreading rumors, excluding the young person, playing nasty jokes, or public humiliation.
- *Cyberbullying* - as the Internet, mobile phone and social media are now part of daily life, bullies are using these digital methods to harass. This can happen at any time and something which the young person can often keep to themselves.
- *Physical Bullying* - this involves physical pinching, punching, kicking, pushing, or damaging personal property.

The story features mostly verbal bullying; however, individual tap along scripts are provided for all four aspects noted above, that the young person can read themselves and tap along with.

Tapping Chart and Guide

A comprehensive tapping chart and guide to all the tapping points is included to help clearly identify the areas to tap on. For those new to EFT I would strongly suggest to use *all* the tapping points in the sequence as noted; however, as confidence in tapping increases, you may use only those tapping points that seem right for you. If, when using some of the tapping points, there is no positive change in how the young person is feeling, then include all tapping points. EFT is very forgiving, and the sequence of where to tap becomes less important as confidence increases, as the focus is to be on the issue being tapped for and not on the sequence of tapping.

Feelings Thermometer (FT)

This is to be used as a guide before and after each round of tapping to determine how the young person is feeling about their issue and how well the tapping is helping. It looks similar to a standard thermometer but has 5 different ways to measure feelings. It measures in numbers from 10 - 0, a thermometer from hot to cold, colors from red to green, emotions from angry to happy and expressions from; being about to explode to being calm and happy.

It is usual for this to start off in or near the distressed measurement and move down to feeling more calm and happy as the tapping helps them feel better.

If it is clearly visible that the young person is very distressed, there is no need to use the feelings thermometer at outset; however, do use it when they starts to feel better.

Tap Along Scripts

The tapping script within the story is listed separately as The Magic Begins, therefore, when you have read the story this script can be used as a stand-alone guide to tap along with.

Additional tapping scripts are provided for each of the four bullying methods noted previously: verbal bullying, intimidating or covert bullying, cyberbullying, and physical bullying. Simply tap along saying the words in the scripts using the tapping points noted. You may refer to the tapping chart and tapping guide at any time.

A blank tapping script is included for the young person to insert their own choice of words or phrases on how they feel about their personal situation and make up their own tapping script. A list of suggested words and phrases are included as a guide. Once confidence increases with EFT, this section could be the most powerful part of the book as it allows the young person to more closely identify with how they really feel about their issue.

Please realize that, as the child more closely identifies with their own issue by their own choice of words and phrases, it has the potential to distress them further; however, if you refer to the previous explanation of *stuck energy*, this is where the magic can really happen. If this is the case, I would strongly suggest to **keep tapping, tapping, tapping** until the young person feels better, as this is what will permanently clear the stuck energy.

Tapping in the Happy's

Included at the end of the rounds of tapping is a positive, uplifting round called *Tapping in the Happy's*. This is to be used when the young person is feeling better and the feelings thermometer is on or near the calm and happy measurement.

Imagination Tapping

This method has been further enhanced by Matrix Reimprinting with EFT, which is an advanced EFT technique that allows the young person to *say or do what they wish they could have said or done* in their bullying experience, all in the safety of their own imagination with the use of their own choice of words and imagery, all whilst tapping on the side of the hand known as the karate chop point.

Tapping Chart and Guide

Tapping is very simple and easy to do and cannot be done wrong, only better.

The actual tapping is done by very lightly tapping with one or two fingers on the tapping points on the face and body as noted in the chart, this is what sends the magical sensations through the body.

It doesn't matter which side of the body is tapped on; choose whichever side is easier to reach and feels most comfortable. If at any time the tapping hurts, simply lighten your touch and move to another tapping point.

The number of times to tap at each point can depend on the statement that is being used, on average tap approximately 7-10 times at each point; however, try not to count the number of times and simply tap along with the statement that is being said.

The starting point is always the KC, karate chop point on the side of the hand, while stating and repeating the main issue three times, ending with a positive statement, for example, 'Although I am being bullied, I know that I am a good person'. Say this statement three times while continually tapping on the KC (side of the hand) point.

After tapping on the KC point and speaking the issue statement three times, out loud or in your mind, the sequence then flows from the top of the body downwards whilst repeating a shorter version of the issue statement or aspects of it. For example, 'Although I am being bullied, I know I am a good person' could be shortened to 'I am being bullied', which is then said at each following tapping point.

The most important part of tapping is *thinking* about, *focusing* on, and *feeling* the issue that is being tapped for. For example, if you are tapping for how you feel about being bullied and are thinking about what time the movie starts, the tapping will not be as effective for bullying as you will be tapping for what time the movie starts! You need to think about, focus on, and feel what it is about bullying for EFT to be most effective.

A key point to look out for is that if after a round or two of tapping, focus cannot be maintained on that issue, then the magic of tapping has probably done its job; therefore, simply move on to the next issue if needed.

One round of tapping is considered as starting from the KC karate chop point and going round on all the following points, twice. This is followed by Tapping in the Happy's and the Imagination Tapping being used at the end.

Use the guide or follow the chart of where and when to tap.

Tapping Guide

All the magical tapping points with illustrations and where to find them on the body are noted here.

The two letter abbreviations will be your guide through all the tapping scripts. If unsure, please see the pictures to accompany this tapping guide.

One full round of tapping covers all the points below with the sequence from the karate chop point (KC) to the gamut point (GA) followed by another round from the top of the head (TH) to the Gamut point (GA), omitting the karate chop (KC) point for the second round.

KC - Karate chop point - the outer side of your hand opposite your thumb - from your little finger to you wrist (either hand)

TH - Top of your head - in the middle of your head

EB - Eyebrow - where your eyebrow starts above the inside corner of your eye, next to the top of your nose (either side of the face)

SE - Side of eye - on the bone on the outer corner of your eye (either side of the face)

UE - Under Eye - in the middle, on the top of the cheekbone

UN - Under the nose - in the dip before your top lip

CH - On your chin - in the dip below your bottom lip

CB - Collarbone - in the middle of your neck, where a knot on a tie may be tied

UA - Under the arm - below your armpit against the side of your body (either side of the body)

WR - The inside of your wrist - where your watch strap may be (either hand)

GA - On your hand - between the knuckles of your little finger and ring finger, about 2cm down in the soft V spot area, known as the Gamut point (either hand)

Tapping Point Illustrations

Below are the illustrations of each of the tapping points which you can refer to at any time.

Note that they are referred to by the abbreviations as stated in the Tapping Guide.

KC—karate chop

The KC—karate chop point. This is the starting point for all tapping and used in imagination tapping. Here you will say the main phrase you wish to tap for three times, whilst continually tapping on this point. For example, 'Even though I am being bullied, I am a good person'.

A shorted phrase is used as you tap on each of the following tapping points, such as 'I am being bullied'.

TH - top of the head

EB - eyebrow

SE - side of eye.

UE - under the eye

UN - under the nose

CH - chin

CB - collarbone

UA - under the arm

WR - inside wrist

GA - gamut

Feelings Thermometer

While tapping for your issue it is important to know how you are feeling about your situation as this is your guide to how well the magic of tapping is helping.

How you feel will generally start off higher or more intense and move down lower to being more relaxed. In some instances, you may start off in the middle of the thermometer, and after a round of tapping the feelings can go up the scale as you think about and focus more on the issue, no different to if you have a sore knee and you think about your knee, it could feel worse. If this happens, *keep tapping* as after this, you should start to feel better and go down the scale.

The feelings thermometer (FT) can be used in five ways to measure how you think or feel about the bullying. Use whichever measurement, or a combination of measurements, that is best for you.

Scale	-	10 to 0
Thermometer	-	Hot to cold
Color	-	Red to Green
Emotions	-	Angry to happy
Expressions	-	I'm about to explode to I am calm and happy

Top of the thermometer—Red

10 - Angry/Crying - I am about to explode

9 - Scared/Stressed - I don't think I can handle it

8 - Frustrated/Helpless - It's all just too much

7 - Anxious/Sad - I am starting to lose it

6 - Worried/Insecure - I can't stop thinking about it

5 - Disappointed/Confused - I don't know how I feel

4 - Irritated/Grumpy - I feel a bit moody

3 - Impatient/Nervous - I might need some help

2 - Unsure/Doubtful - I don't feel right

1 - Positive/Hopeful - Things are OK

0 - Happy/Relaxed - I am calm and happy

Bottom of the thermometer—Green

The Magic Begins

Jessica was feeling very worried. Why, oh, why did they have to pick on her? She is a lovely person, yet a certain group of people insisted on teasing her and making her feel really bad.

She used to love going to school, but she didn't want to go there anymore, and at times, she felt like she just wanted to run far away from that place.

She sat on the floor in her room not wanting to get up and have her dinner. She was crying but didn't want anyone to hear her because she knew that there was nothing anyone could do about it. In fact, by doing something, she thought that it would only get worse, and the bullies would just tease her even more, and that was the very last thing she wanted.

The friends she had were all very kind, and she could talk to them sometimes as she knew they wouldn't tell if she asked them not to, but adults see things differently and cannot possibly understand what she is going through.

She heard footsteps coming down the hall towards her room, and Mum called Jessica for the third time to come and have her dinner. Jessica managed to find her voice and called back saying that she wasn't feeling hungry and that she would get something a little later.

What am I to do? thought Jessica, with her head in her hands. *Maybe I will pretend to be sick tomorrow so I don't have to go in to school.* But then she remembered that she had a test in the afternoon which she hadn't been able to think about at all. *I'm doomed,* she thought. Just then there was a light knock on her door. 'Are you all right?' asked Mum. 'I'm fine,' said Jessica, 'just revising for my test tomorrow.' She had lied to Mum and wasn't at all proud of it, but it was the first thing that came out of her mouth, and besides, what else could she say at that moment? She was trying to revise but couldn't stop the thoughts of what the bullies might say or do to her tomorrow.

Her door opened slightly, and Mum peeked round. 'I know you're not fine,' said Mum. 'What is it?'

'Go away,' Jessica said in a more raised voice. 'I don't want to talk about it.' As much as Mum wanted to respect what Jessica had said, she also knew that she hadn't been her usual happy self for some time, and she was feeling quite concerned about her. She opened the door a little more and gently went into her room and sat down on the floor next to Jessica. Jessica turned her head away so that Mum couldn't see that she had been crying, and Mum picked up Jessica's hand and lightly started to tap on the side of her hand, the karate chop (KC) point, while saying,

'I know there's something going on that you don't want to talk about, but that's all right. You don't have to say anything until you want to, and you know that you are a great girl.

'I know that you are worried and that it might be something going on at school that is difficult for you to talk about it, but it's OK, you are still a great girl.

'It might be something going on at school that's bothering you, but you are a great girl, and I love you very much.'

Well, that did it. Jessica burst into floods of tears.

Jessica was feeling worried

Mum gave her a hug and then told her about EFT and said that it's a magical way to help her feel better, and that it worked by saying what was on her mind and tapping at the same time, and asked if she wanted to give it a try.

'Maybe', shrugged Jessica. 'What do I need to do?' said Jessica, not really paying much attention. 'Just say what is happening and how you feel about it and follow along with the tapping,' said Mum.

'All right,' said Jessica. 'If you like, I can give it a try, but I'm not sure that it will help any.'

'Would you like to tell me what is worrying you?' asked Mum.

Jessica stopped for a moment and thought if she really wanted to tell Mum but was curious about EFT being magical, as Mum had said, so she told her that there were people at school that are making fun of her and calling her names and that they sometimes take her books away and hide them. Jessica started to feel sad again. 'And I don't want to go to school anymore,' she cried.

'Well, that's not nice at all,' said Mum. 'But I'm glad you have told me, and it is a good start for using EFT. Let's start by using the feelings thermometer [FT] for measuring how you feel about it.' The FT was all the way to the top on the red, which was no surprise as Jessica was very upset.

Mum asked Jessica to follow along with her and repeat what was being said and tap on the same places on her own self that Mum was tapping on herself. If Jessica got too unhappy to speak, then it was OK to just nod with what was being said.

Jessica repeated and followed each of the sentences and tapping exactly as Mum said and did.

KC - 'There are people at school that are making fun of me and calling me names, and it's very worrying, but I'm a good person.'

KC - 'Those people are bullies and are making fun of me and sometimes take my books away, and I don't know why because I am a great person.'

KC - 'They make me feel like I don't want to go to school anymore, but I know I'm a good person.'

'I'm scared,' cried Jessica. 'Why can't they leave me alone?'

Mum then started to lightly tap on the other points and asked Jessica to copy and repeat what she said and did next.

TH - 'The bullies scare me.'

EB - 'They call me names.'

SE - 'Why can't they leave me alone?'

UE - 'I don't want to go to school.'

UN - 'Why do they pick on me?'

CH - 'It's very hurtful.'

CB - 'I want them to stop.'

UA - 'The bullies call me names, and I want it to stop.'

WR - 'I don't want to go to school.'

GA - 'I am very scared and unhappy.'

They did this another time, saying,

TH - 'The bullies make fun of me.'

EB - 'They call me names.'

SE - 'They're horrible names.'

UE - 'And I don't deserve it.'

UN - 'I don't know why they pick on me.'

CH - 'I haven't done anything wrong.'

CB - 'I want them to stop.'

UA - 'I don't want to go to school.'

WR - 'I can't concentrate.'

GA - 'And it's very worrying.'

Jessica looked up at Mum and said, 'I'm worried about what they will say or do next, and I didn't want to tell anyone because it might make it worse. They would just get even angrier at me for telling, and I don't know what to do. You won't tell, will you, Mum?'

'Let's see how we get on with EFT first,' said Mum. 'We're not finished yet. How are you feeling, and where is the feelings thermometer at now?'

Jessica looked at it and thought about it, then decided that it had gone down and was now in the middle, which surprised her as only a little while ago it was all the way at the top on the red!

'You're doing very well,' said Mum. 'Yes,' said Jessica. 'It's strange, but I am feeling a little bit better. Can we do it again?' said Jessica.

Mum asked Jessica to tap along and repeat what she was saying.

KC - 'I am worried about what the bullies will say or do next, and I don't want to tell anyone because it might make it worse, but I'm a great girl.'

KC - 'They would just get angrier at me for telling, and I don't know what to do, but I am doing the best I can.'

KC - 'I worried about telling anyone because I'm scared of what they might do next, but I am a good person.'

34

Mum and Jessica went round the tapping points again.

TH - 'I'm afraid to tell anyone.'

EB - 'They might get angrier with me.'

SE - 'I don't know what they will say or do next.'

UE - 'I feel very worried about it.'

UN - 'Why do they pick on me?'

CH - 'I don't want to tell anyone because it might make it worse.'

CB - 'But I want them to stop.'

UA - 'I don't know what to do about it.'

WR - 'I am scared.'

GA - 'They might get angrier with me.'

Mum asked Jessica if she knew where the scared feeling was in her body. Was it in her tummy or her head or maybe somewhere else? 'I feel it in my tummy,' she said. 'It feels like I might want to be sick.'

'We can use that in the tapping if you like,' said Mum. 'It could make it go away.'

'All right, we can try,' said Jessica.

They tapped again, and this time Mum asked Jessica to repeat what she said about where she felt the scared feeling.

TH - 'I feel the scared feeling in my tummy.'

EB - 'I feel like I might want to be sick.'

SE - 'The bullies make me feel like this.'

UE - 'Because they scare me.'

UN - 'I feel sick in my tummy.'

CH - 'Because the bullies make fun of me and call me names.'

CB - 'And it makes my tummy hurt.'

UA - 'I don't want to eat anything.'

WR - 'I want to feel better.'

GA - 'I want to stop feeling sick.'

'Wow!' said Jessica. 'This tapping is magic. I am feeling much better.' As she told Mum that the FT was almost down to the green.

'That's wonderful,' said Mum. 'Shall we try *tapping in the happy's* now?'

'Yes, please,' said Jessica quite excitedly now.

'All right, follow me again,' said Mum.

Mum taps on Jessica

KC - 'Even though I am still feeling a little worried about what the bullies might say or do, I am a great person and there's no one quite like me.'

KC - 'Even though they might make fun of me and call me names, they are only names after all.'

KC - 'Even though I'm not sure about telling on them, I might be changing my mind.'

TH - 'The bullies make fun of me.'

EB - 'But it's only names.'

SE - 'Names can't really hurt anyone unless you want them to.'

UE - 'I can decide to be happy anyway.'

UN - 'People still like me.'

CH - 'It doesn't matter what people say.'

CB - 'I am me, and I am awesome.'

UA - 'They're silly names anyway and don't really mean anything.'

WR - 'I can choose not to listen to them.'

GA - 'If I don't listen, then the words can't hurt me.'

Mum asked Jessica to take a slow deep breath in and slowly blow it out. 'That feels so much better now,' said Jessica.

Mum told Jessica how well she had done with the tapping, and although she was feeling better, there was one more thing she wanted to ask Jessica to try called imagination tapping. 'That sounds interesting,' said Jessica. 'What is it about?'

'It's about using your imagination with the tapping to help you feel even better,' Mum said. 'Imagine you can see yourself in school and the bullies are teasing you, can you do that?'

'Yes, I can,' said Jessica. 'That's easy.'

'Well,' said Mum, 'if that you in your imagination, being bullied in the school, could say anything at all to the bullies, what might she say if she knew that she would not get into trouble for it and also know that the bullies would listen to her? It's all pretending, but let's see if she would want to say or do anything. Just close your eyes and tap on your KC point while you do this in your imagination,' said Mum.

'That sounds like a fun game,' said Jessica, and she imagined the picture of looking at herself standing in the school, seeing and hearing what the bullies were saying to her, and how she might have felt about it.

'Ask that you in the picture what she might like to say to the bullies,' suggested Mum.

'All right,' said Jessica, 'that me being bullied in my imagination would like to tell them that they are being horrible bullies and how they make me feel angry and scared and to tell them to stop doing it.'

'Wonderful,' said Mum. 'See if you can see that happening in your mind now.'

Jessica saw in her mind the picture of herself telling the bullies off and saying that they shouldn't bully her because it makes her feel bad. She let them know how she wasn't able to concentrate at school or sleep much at night for worrying about it and how her grades were suffering. She told them how it made her feel sick and she couldn't eat, and she then decided that she wanted the bullies in her picture to say sorry to her and the teachers to come in and give them all detention for a whole week.

Jessica uses imagination tapping

Jessica opened her eyes and told Mum all that she had imagined in her mind and how much better she was feeling now and asked if she had been silly to let the things that people had said to her make her feel so bad. 'Not at all,' said Mum. 'I'm sure it must have been very worrying for you, but I am glad that you are feeling better about it now.'

'I am,' said Jessica. 'This is like magic,' giggled Jessica.

Mum asked, 'Can you feel that much better feeling?'

'Yes, I can,' said Jessica. 'I feel it all over. It feels warm and tingly.'

'That's good,' Mum said. 'Place your hand on your heart and see if you can put that warm and tingly feeling there and know that if you feel sad about it again, you know just where to find that good feeling.'

'That's a great idea,' said Jessica, as she took a minute to close her eyes again, place her hand on her heart and felt that warm and tingly feeling in her heart, and all over her body.

Jessica opened her eyes. 'I'm hungry,' she said. 'Can we have some dinner now?'

The Magic Story Script

TAP ALONG SCRIPT

This tapping script can be used by itself apart from the main story by reading it out loud to the young person, or the young person can read this themselves.

It is written as if the young person is doing the tapping themselves, so simply tap along on the points noted saying the words below out loud or in your mind. Do as many rounds of tapping as you need to allow the magic of EFT to really work.

First round of tapping

KC - There are people at school that are making fun of me and calling me names and it's very worrying, but I'm a great person.

KC - Those people are bullies and are making fun of me and I can't concentrate, and I don't know why because I am a great person.

KC - They make me feel like I don't want to go to school anymore, but I know I'm a good person.

TH - The bullies scare me.

EB - They call me names.

SE - Why can't they leave me alone?

UE - I don't want to go to school.

UN - Why do they pick on me?

CH - It's very hurtful.

CB - I want them to stop.

UA - The bullies call me names, and I want it to stop.

WR - I don't want to go to school.

GA - I am very scared and unhappy.

TH - The bullies make fun of me.

EB - They call me names.

SE - They are horrible names.

UE - And I don't deserve it.

UN - I don't know why they pick on me.

CH - I haven't done anything wrong.

CB - I want them to stop.

UA - I don't want to go to school.

WR - I can't concentrate.

GA - And it's very worrying.

Next round of tapping

KC - I am worried about what the bullies will say or do next, and I don't want to tell anyone because it might make it worse, but I'm a great person.

KC - They would just get angrier at me for telling, and I don't know what to do, but I am doing the best I can.

KC - I worried about telling anyone because I'm scared of what they might do next, but I am a good person.

TH - I'm afraid to tell anyone.

EB - They might get angrier with me.

SE - I don't know what they will say or do next.

UE - I feel very worried about it.

UN - Why do they pick on me?

CH - I don't want to tell anyone because it might make it worse.

CB - But I want them to stop.

UA - I don't know what to do about it.

WR - I am scared.

GA - They might get angrier with me.

TH - I feel the scared feeling in my tummy.

EB - I feel like I might want to be sick.

SE - The bullies make me feel like this.

UE - Because they scare me.

UN - I feel sick in my tummy.

CH - Because the bullies make fun of me and call me names.

CB - And it makes my tummy hurt.

UA - I don't want to eat anything.

WR - I want to feel better.

GA - I want to stop feeling sick.

Tapping in the Happy's

KC - Even though I am still feeling a little worried about what the bullies might say or do, I am a great person and there's no one quite like me.

KC - Even though they might make fun of me and call me names, they are only names after all.

KC - Even though I'm not sure about telling anyone, I might be changing my mind.

TH - The bullies make fun of me.

EB - But it's only names.

SE - Names can't really hurt anyone unless you want them to.

UE - I can decide to be happy anyway.

UN - People still like me.

CH - It doesn't matter what people say.

CB - I am me, and I am awesome.

UA - They're silly names anyway and don't really mean anything.

WR - I can choose not to listen to them.

GA - If I don't listen to them, then the words can't hurt me.

Take a slow, relaxing deep breath in and slowly blow it out again.

Imagination tapping

Tap on the KC point while you do the following:

Close your eyes and imagine that you can see yourself in school and the bullies are teasing you. In your imagination, if you could say anything to the bullies, what might you say if you knew that you would be safe and not get into trouble for it and the bullies would listen to you?

See and hear in your mind the picture of you telling the bullies exactly how you feel about it and saying that they should stop bullying you because it hurts and upsets you. Let them know that you are not able to concentrate at school or sleep much at night for worrying about it and how it makes you feel sick and you can't eat. See the bullies in your imagination saying sorry and the teachers come in and giving them all detention, or anything else that needs to happen just for you. It's your own imagination and anything can happen here. Keep tapping on the KC point until you have finished and feel much better, then open your eyes.

When this has been done, close your eyes again for a moment, place your hand on your heart and try to put that *much better feeling* in your heart in whatever way seems right for you, knowing that if you feel sad about it again, you know where to find that good feeling.

The author would like to say a personal 'very well done' to you for helping yourself feel better and taking back your own self-power.`

EFT Magic for Intimidating or Covert Bullying

TAP ALONG SCRIPT

This form of bullying is often done behind people's back and consists of the bully spreading rumors, excluding someone from joining in, playing nasty jokes, or public humiliation.

This tapping script can be used by itself in any intimidating or covert bullying situation and can be read out loud to the young person or the young person can read it themselves. Simply tap along on the points noted saying the words below out loud or in your mind. Do as many rounds of tapping as you need to allow the magic of EFT to really work.

It is written as if the young person is doing the tapping themselves, therefore where possible, try to include any words that are being said to you personally, within the tapping script.

First round of tapping

KC - People are spreading rumors about me and saying nasty things, but I know I am a good person.

KC - They are very hurtful and untrue things, but some friends are believing them, but I am still a nice person.

KC - I don't know how to make them stop, and I don't want to go to school, but I know I'm a good person.

TH - The bullies say horrible things.

EB - They are spreading nasty rumors about me.

SE - It makes me very angry.

UE - I don't want to go to school.

UN - It's not true, but no one believes me.

CH - I want them to stop.

CB - Some of my friends don't want to know me because of what they are saying.

UA - They don't like me.

WR - The bullies spread nasty rumors and are saying horrible things.

GA - I am very scared and annoyed.

TH - I feel very angry and hurt by it.

EB - People are laughing at me.

SE - They make fun of me behind my back.

UE - I'm afraid to say anything.

UN - It's very hurtful.

CH - I'm afraid.

CB - They are bigger and stronger than me, and there are more of them.

UA - I don't want to go to school.

WR - I can't concentrate.

GA - They do things that make me look stupid.

Next round of tapping

KC - It hurts being made fun of, but I am a great person.

KC - I don't know what to do about it, but I am doing what I can.

KC - Even though I worry about what they might do, I am a good person.

TH - I am still angry and worried.

EB - I don't know how to stop it.

SE - They do it behind my back.

UE - They make me look stupid in front of others.

UN - They say hurtful things to me.

CH - I get excluded from things.

CB - Everyone laughs about it.

UA - It hurts to know these things are being said.

WR - No one will let me join in with them.

GA - They don't want to know me.

TH - They think I'm stupid.

EB - They exclude me from things.

SE - The bullies make me feel like this.

UE - What they say makes me sad.

UN - I want it to stop.

CH - The bullies talk about me behind my back.

CB - And it makes me feel lonely.

UA - I'd like to join in.

WR - I want to feel better.

GA - I want to be able to join in and have lots of friends.

Tapping in the Happy's

KC - Even though I still feel a bit angry about what the bullies say, I am a great person and there's no one quite like me.

KC - They make me look stupid in front of others, but I know what I am good at.

KC - They try to make me feel small, but I know it's only if I let them.

TH - The bullies laugh at me behind my back.

EB - But I know I must be good at something.

SE - People can't be good at everything.

UE - I can decide how I feel and can choose to be happy anyway.

UN - Maybe I can laugh it off.

CH - It doesn't matter what people say.

CB - I am me, and I am awesome.

UA - I know it's not true, and that's what matters.

WR - There are lots of things I can do instead.

GA - People like me just the way I am.

Take a slow, relaxing deep breath in and slowly blow it out again.

Imagination tapping

Tap on the KC point while you do the following:

Close your eyes and imagine that you can see yourself where the bullies are talking about you behind your back or you are being excluded from things. Hear what the bullies say or do to make you look or feel stupid. In your imagination see yourself speaking to the bullies and, if you could say anything to them, what might you say if you knew that you would be safe, not get into trouble for it, and the bullies would listen to you?

See and hear in your mind the picture of you speaking with the bullies and letting them know *exactly* how it makes you feel.

See the bullies' reaction in your picture, maybe saying sorry, or if you need to bring someone else into your picture that can help you deal with the bullies such as a teacher or parent or anyone and anything else that needs to happen just for you, it's your own imagination. You are safe, and anything can happen here. Keep tapping on the KC point until you have finished and feel better, then open your eyes.

When this has been done, close your eyes again for a moment, place your hand on your heart, and try to put that better feeling in your heart in whatever way seems right for you, knowing that if you feel hurt about it again, you know where to find that good feeling.

EFT Magic for Cyberbullying

TAP ALONG SCRIPT

Bullying by using digital methods such as the Internet, mobile phones or social media to harass others is increasing, and can have serious effects on health and well-being. This frequently happens outside of school and is often kept quiet about due to feeling as if there is little to no control over it.

This tapping script can be used by itself in any cyberbullying situation and can be read out loud to the young person or the young person can read it themselves. Simply tap along on the points noted saying the words below out loud or in your mind. Do as many rounds of tapping as you need to allow the magic of EFT to really work.

This script is written as if the young person is doing the tapping themselves, therefore where possible, try to include any words that are being said to you personally, within the tapping script.

First round of tapping

KC - Even though I'm getting nasty messages and being threatened, I am a good person.

KC - I can get these messages a lot, they just don't leave me alone, and I don't know why because I am a nice person.

KC - Even though these messages are wearing me down, I know I am a good person.

TH - I'm getting nasty messages.

EB - They are saying hurtful things.

SE - They threaten me.

UE - They say if I don't do something, they will get even nastier.

UN - They text me at night or when I'm alone.

CH - I'm very scared.

CB - They are horrible messages.

UA - I want it to stop.

WR - I don't want to read them, but I have to.

GA - I'm scared to do anything.

TH - These nasty horrible messages.

EB - I don't know what to do.

SE - I don't want to do what they say.

UE - But what if I don't?

UN - I don't want it to get worse.

CH - No one knows about it.

CB - They say not to tell or it will get worse.

UA - I'm very scared.

WR - These nasty messages.

GA - It's very hurtful.

Next round of tapping

KC - Even though I am worried about what will happen next and I don't want to tell anyone because it might make it worse, I'm a great person.

KC - I can get these messages any time, and I don't know what to do, but I am coping the best I can.

KC - Even though I am scared about telling because of what they might say next, I know I can get support if I ask.

TH - I'm very scared.

EB - I get threatening messages.

SE - They tell me to do things.

UE - I am very worried about it.

UN - I don't want to reply, but sometimes I have to.

CH - They just don't stop.

CB - They say horrible and hurtful things.

UA - I don't know what to do about it.

WR - I don't want it to get any worse.

GA - They threaten me.

TH - I feel the scared feeling in my chest.

EB - I feel like I want to scream.

SE - The bullies make me feel like this.

UE - Because of these messages.

UN - These horrible messages.

CH - The bullies keep sending these to me.

CB - It keeps me awake at night.

UA - It makes my head spin.

WR - I'm very worried.

GA - I want them to stop right now.

Tapping in the Happy's

KC - Even though I am still feeling a bit scared about getting these nasty messages, I am a good person.

KC - Even though they say horrible things, they are only words after all.

KC - Even though I'm not sure what to do, I'm sure someone is there to help me.

TH - The bullies send me messages.

EB - But it's only words.

SE - I can choose not to believe them.

UE - I can ask someone else to delete it.

UN - If I don't know about it, it can't hurt me.

CH - They can't make me do anything I don't want to do.

CB - I am me, and I am awesome.

UA - The bullies don't have anything better to do.

WR - I can choose not to let it hurt me.

GA - If I don't respond, then it can't hurt me.

Take a slow, relaxing deep breath in and slowly blow it out again.

Imagination tapping

Tap on the KC point while you do the following:

Close your eyes and imagine that you are looking at a message that you have received. In your imagination, see yourself in a safe place where you can say anything to the bullies. What might you say if you knew that the bullies would listen to you and that you would not get into more trouble with them for saying it?

See and hear in your mind the picture of you telling the bullies *exactly* how you feel and why they shouldn't do what they do. Let them know how you are not able to sleep and how their words keep going round and round in your head, how you are afraid or anything else that you feel. See the bullies in your picture maybe saying sorry to you, and if needed, bring someone into your picture that can support you that the bullies would listen to. It can be anyone. Say anything else that needs to happen just for you. It's your own imagination and anything can happen here. Keep tapping on the KC point until you have finished, and when you feel better, slowly open your eyes.

When this has been done, close your eyes again for a moment, place your hand on your heart, and try to put that *much better feeling* in your heart in whatever way seems right for you, knowing that if you feel hurt by it again, you know where to find that good feeling.

EFT Magic for Physical Bullying

TAP ALONG SCRIPT

Physical bullying this involves physical pinching, punching, kicking, pushing, or damaging personal property.

This form of bullying can be difficult to stop. In previous situations, as self-confidence increases the bullies will leave someone alone as they get no reaction.

With physical bullying, although you may feel better, it may not stop the physical harm straight away as it's not easy to pretend it doesn't hurt. However, as you gain in self-confidence and find the power to stand up to the bullies the bullies may then back down.

I would also encourage the use of other resources in conjunction with EFT tapping to help with physical bullying situations.

This tapping script can be used by itself in any physical bullying situation and can be read out loud to the young person or the young person can read it themselves. Simply tap along on the points noted saying the words below out loud or in your mind, or include your own words at any point in the tapping script. Do as many rounds of tapping as you need to allow the magic of EFT to really work.

This script is written as if the young person is doing the tapping themselves therefore where possible, try to include any words that are being said to you personally, within the tapping script.

First round of tapping

KC - Even though the bullies push and kick me, I am a great person.

KC - They never leave me alone, and I don't know why because I am a good person.

KC - Even though the bullies hit me, I know people still like me.

TH - I am getting hit.

EB - They are always picking on me.

SE - They kick and punch me because they don't like me.

UE - The bullies hit me.

UN - I'm afraid to go anywhere.

CH - If I see them out, I go the other way.

CB - The bullies keep hitting me.

UA - They wreck my stuff.

WR - They are big bullies.

GA - I am very scared of them.

TH - The bullies keep hitting me.

EB - They always pick on me.

SE - They hit and punch me.

UE - Sometimes I cry.

UN - Sometimes I get angry.

CH - The bullies hit me.

CB - I can't fight back; they're bigger than me.

UA - I'm very scared.

WR - They try to beat me up.

GA - I'm scared to be alone.

Next round of tapping

KC - Even though the bullies hit and punch me, I know that I'm a good person.

KC - Although the bullies wreck my stuff, I am kind to others.

KC - Even though I am scared of what they might do, I can believe in myself.

TH - I'm still scared.

EB - They kick and punch me.

SE - They beat me up, and it hurts.

UE - I can't fight back.

UN - I'm not allowed to fight back.

CH - They are bigger than me.

CB - It would only make things worse.

UA - I would get hit even more.

WR - The bullies hit me.

GA - They wreck my stuff.

TH - I am scared to speak up.

EB - I can't defend myself.

SE - The bullies hate me.

UE - That's why they hit me.

UN - They single me out.

CH - I'm not able to fight back.

CB - The bullies hit and kick me.

UA - It hurts me physically and mentally.

WR - I don't want to go out anywhere.

GA - And I want it to stop.

Tapping in the Happy's

KC - Even though the bullies hit me, I know that I am a good person.

KC - Even though they wreck my stuff, it doesn't have to happen to me.

KC - Even though I'm not sure what to do, I know I have lots of support.

TH - The bullies hit me.

EB - That's what bullies do.

SE - They pick on me.

UE - If I become strong, they could leave me alone.

UN - I can walk away.

CH - I know I can be strong.

CB - I don't need to react to them.

UA - There is help and support for me.

WR - I could choose to feel better.

GA - What if I started feeling better right now?

Take a slow, relaxing deep breath in and slowly blow it out again.

Imagination tapping

Tap on the KC point while you do the following:

Close your eyes and imagine a situation where the bullies have physically harmed you in any way.

In your imagination, see yourself in a safe place where you can say anything to the bullies. What might you say if you knew that the bullies would listen to you and that you would not get into more trouble with them for saying it to them?

See and hear in your mind the picture of you telling the bullies *exactly* how you feel about it, how their actions physically and mentally hurt you, and why they should stop what they are doing. Let them know the hurt you feel and maybe ask how they would feel if it happened to them. Maybe see the bullies in your picture saying sorry to you, and if needed, imagine someone into your picture that can support you that the bullies would listen to. It can be anyone. Say anything else that needs to happen just for you. It's your own imagination and anything can happen here. Keep tapping on the KC point until you have finished, and when you feel better, slowly open your eyes.

When this has been done, close your eyes again for a moment, place your hand on your heart, and try to put that *much better feeling* in your heart in whatever way seems right for you, knowing that if you feel hurt by it again, you know where to find that good feeling.

Discover the Full Magic of EFT

BLANK TAP ALONG GUIDE AND SCRIPT

Young people can often struggle to find the words to describe their feelings; therefore, noted below is a suggested list of words and phrases which can be used to make up your own tapping script to fit your own personal bullying situation. Use any that are appropriate to you.

You can use the blank script below as a guide or go back over any previous scripts and replace some of the words in those scripts with a more detailed explanation of your event in your own words.

Use your imagination and get in touch with your own personal situation and say *exactly* what is happening to you as you tap along, in your mind or out loud, and allow the magic of EFT to really work.

Suggested phrases

These additional phrases could be used with the initial start-up statement when tapping on the KC point or as shortened phrases throughout the tapping.

- I hate being bullied.
- I'm very scared of them and what they might do.
- They call me names.
- I don't deserve it.
- I feel useless.
- I get a hiding
- Whatever I do, they still find me.
- I'm afraid of being alone.
- I can't get away from them.
- I don't know what I've done.
- They don't let me join in.
- I don't want to log in.
- I can't read my email. It's very scary.
- There's nothing I can do.
- Why do they pick on me?
- I get beaten up.
- I want to stay home.
- I can't go out anywhere.
- I want to run and hide.
- They laugh and make fun at me.
- They verbally abuse me.
- They know where I live.
- The way they look at me scares me.
- They are bigger than me.

- There must be something wrong with me.

Suggested words

A) abuse, afraid, aggressive, alone, annoy, assault, attack, angry, avoid, airhead.

B) beat up, bother, bruiser, betray, burden.

C) cow, cheat, coward, conflict, chicken, creepy, cruel, crushed, criticize.

D) despair, devastate, die, disaster, dishonest, dead, disrespect, deceive, destroy, dirty, disgusting, doomed.

E) effect, embarrass, emotional, evil, empty, exclude.

F) failure, fat, fear, force, frightened, fault, freak, fake, frustrated.

G) gang, gossip, gay, goth, grossed-out, guilt.

H) harass, hide, hopeless, homo, hostile, humiliate, hurt, hate.

I) ignorant, ignore, improper, innocent, insult, irresponsible, idiot, insane, intimidate.

J) jealous, judge, jerk.

K) kicked, knockdown, knucklehead.

L) liar, loser, loopy, lousy, lowlife.

M) malicious, mean, mad, messed up, miserable, mistrust, muppet.

N) nervous, nuisance, nerd, nasty, nuts.

O) offensive, out-of-line, outcast, overwhelm, overweight, odd.

P) pain, pig, picked on, pity, prey, punched, pushing, put-down, pinhead, pathetic, phony.

Q) quake, quarrel, quirky.

R) rude, rank, rant, regret, rage, resent, reject.

S) selfish, shaken up, sad, shorty, shock, shout, shove, struggle, suffer, stupid, shy, spiteful, scream, spoon.

T) target, tease, threaten, terrify, thug, torment, trauma, trick, tart, trapped.

U) ugly, unfair, unreasonable, unkind, useless.

V) vicious, victim, violent.

W) warning, weary, wicked, worry, wound, wannabe, wrong, whale, witch, worthless.

Y) yelling, yellow-belly.

Blank tapping script

Insert any of the above words or phrases or make up your own about your personal bullying situation.

Whilst tapping on the KC point, say the start-up statement three times.

For example, Even though (*the bullies make fun of me*) I am a great person

KC - Even though (*say what is happening*), I am a great person.

KC - Even though (*say what is happening*), I am a good person.

KC - Even though (*say what is happening*), I believe in myself.

In a few words, say what is happening and how it makes you *feel*, whilst tapping on the points as noted below from TH to GA, use any of the words from the suggested words list or make up your own.

For example, I feel angry.

TH -

EB -

SE -

UE -

UN -

CH -

CB -

UA -

WR -

GA -

Repeat from TH to GA.

Note that this makes up one full round of tapping.

Repeat another full round if needed from TH to GA points, doing two rounds of tapping in all.

Tapping in the Happy's

Below are some additional suggested words or phrases for Tapping in the Happy's.

- Words can't hurt me.
- I am awesome.
- I like me just how I am.
- Sticks and stones.
- I don't have to change for them to like me.
- I can choose not to listen.
- If I don't react they will stop.
- I don't need them.
- I'm not like that.
- I have my own circle of friends.
- I can walk away.
- I am supported.

- People care about me.
- There is always someone to help me.
- I can be strong.
- Lots of people like me.
- I can choose to be confident and happy.
- I am amazing.
- I love myself.
- I believe in me.
- I will try not to react.
- Bullies are stupid.
- Friends are out there, I just need to find them.

Say the negative feeling followed by a positive statement.

For example, Even though (*the bullies call me names*), I choose to be happy.

KC - Even though (*negative statement*), I love myself.

KC - Even though (*negative statement*), I choose to be happy.

KC - Even though (*negative statement*), I am supported.

Use this section to say a few positive statements. Refer to any of the previous Tapping in the Happy's sections, insert your own choice of words or select any from the above list, or you can even mix them up as to what feels right for you.

For example you may say, *I choose not to listen, I can be strong* and tap on all the points from TH to GA.

TH -

EB -

SE -

UE -

UN -

CH -

CB -

UA -

WR -

GA -

If needed, repeat from TH to GA.

Imagination tapping

Tap on the KC point while you do the following:

Close your eyes and imagine a situation where the bullies are doing what they do to you.

In your imagination, see yourself in a safe place where you can say *anything* to the bullies. What might you say if you knew that the bullies would listen to you and that you would not get into trouble with them or anyone else? You can bring anyone into your picture that you think would be of help to you, real or imaginary, i.e. a teacher, a parent, or any superhero. You can imagine yourself bigger and taller or the bullies smaller, if that helps you.

There is no script for this. It's about using your own imagination to deal with the situation how you wish you could, in any way you could, yet all in the safety of your own imagination and while you tap on your KC point.

Take as long as you need to and stop when you feel it's completed.

Once you feel better, place your hand over your heart, and place that good feeling in your heart so you know where you can find it at any time.

Conclusion

EFT offers children a way to deal with the effects of bullying at anytime, anywhere and provides a way for the young person to *do* something about the situation and remove that helpless feeling.

EFT can be done on the spot, the moment a bully says or does something that cause distress. They no longer need to suffer the anxious and have their thoughts turn over and over in their mind while they wait to seek professional help.

Using EFT while feeling distress about being bullied on a regular basis will help to generate a feeling of personal power and take away the helpless feelings associated with it.

Using EFT will improve the ability to focus more in school, fit in with peers and make friends. Children will be able to sleep better and gain a new level of self-esteem. They may even think of the bully in a different way, possibly even realizing that the bully themselves may be hurting and gain a level of understanding of *why*.

Bullying may always exist somewhere in some form or another, and it is the author's hope that this book gets distributed far and wide to find and help all those in need that are going through any form of bullying, and gives them the tools to find their own confidence so that bullying will no longer have any impact for those on the receiving end.

The audio of the story and tapping scripts can be found on the website along with a video demonstration of how and where to tap.

I hope you have enjoyed discovering the magic of EFT for Bullying.

Look out for other titles coming up in this series:

- Discover the Magic of EFT for Anxiety

- Discover the Magic of EFT for Anger

- Discover the Magic of EFT for Parental Separation

- Discover the Magic of EFT for Exam Stress

and more.

About the Author

International advanced EFT practitioner EFT trainer and advanced Matrix Reimprinting practitioner, Debby Guddee has been working with adults and children using EFT for many years with a wide range of issues.

Born in the United Kingdom, her passion for helping others started with hands-on energy healing therapies. Debby has since travelled extensively and studied EFT via Gary Craig (the founder of EFT) and Matrix Reimprinting via Karl Dawson (the founder of Matrix Reimprinting). She has also studied Systematic and Touch for Health Kinesiology for many years, along with Kinergetics, an energy form of Kinesiology.

She regularly holds EFT trainings in New Zealand, where she now resides, and has her own private EFT practice.

Debby has worked as a senior business analyst for many years on multimillion-dollar national projects in the United Kingdom, Isle of Man and New Zealand.

She is a mother to one daughter and has one grandson and writes successful children's picture books with her daughter, Melissa Rodrigues, where their first title, My Favorite Hugs, was voted one of the most notable children's books of 2013 by Shelf Unbound.

For further information or to download audios or video demonstrations, please go to:

www.debbyguddee.com

Also find Debby on Facebook

For further information about Matrix Reimprinting with EFT go to:

www.matrixreimprinting.com

CPSIA information can be obtained
at www.ICGtesting.com
Printed in the USA
LVOW12s2234310517

536513LV00006B/369/P

9 781500 195281